- and tonnes more coolness besides!

Let's not waste any more time – here are the 101 coolest things not to miss in Reykjavik!

1. Climb the Tower of Hallgrimskirkja

Hallgrimskirkja is quite possibly the most iconic building in the whole country. Standing tall at a height of 73 metres, this is actually the tallest church in Iceland, and the sixth tallest structure in the country. Taking in the unique architectural style of the Lutheran church is rewarding enough, but you can also climb to the very top of the tower where you will experience a killer view of all of Reykjavik.

(Hallgrímstorg 101; www.hallgrimskirkja.is)

2. Immerse Yourself in Local History at an Open Air Museum

If you are fascinated by history but are not so engaged by stuffy museums, you might want to try a museum experience with a difference at Arbaejarsfan. This is an open-air museum that is dedicated to providing insight into the lives, homes, and work of Icelandic people in centuries gone by. Instead of artefacts behind glass, you'll find recreations of life as it was in history. As you walk around, you can explore areas such as the Blacksmith's House, a stable, a boy scout hut, a farm, and lots more besides.

(4, 110, Kistuhylur; http://borgarsogusafn.is/en/arbaer-open-air-museum)

3. Take a Steam Bath in the Blue Lagoon

While the geothermal spa of the Blue Lagoon is not located exactly in Reykjavik, it isn't far from the city, is easy to get to, and it's well worth the visit. In fact, it has been called the best medical spa in the world by Conde Nast. One of the highlights of any visit that has to be a luxurious steam bath, which is also powered by the local geothermal energy. It's the best place in Iceland to relax, unwind, and get over any unwanted jetlag.

(www.bluelagoon.com)

4. Get Cultural on Culture Night

Culture Night is definitely one of the most fun nights of the year on the city's calendar. It takes place every year in August, and it's on this night that you'll find tonnes of activities, parties, and festivities all around the city's streets. The event marks the start of the cultural year and many galleries, museums, and event spaces launch their programme for the cultural year on this night. You'll find music performances, dance shows, impromptu plays, and pop-up art exhibitions in Reykjavik, as well as 100,000 people joining in with the fun.

(http://culturenight.is)

5. Eat Lots of Yummy Hot Spring Rye Bread

Iceland isn't exactly famous on the culinary map of the world, but that is not to say that there isn't plenty of deliciousness for you to try while you're in the country, and something that we can't get enough of is hot spring rye bread. The reason it's specifically called hot spring rye bread is because the loaves are steamed within wooden casks that are buried in the ground of a hot spring. The flavour is dark, dense, sweet, and we think it's totally yummy.

6. Have a Whale Watching Adventure

People who visit Iceland for its spectacular nature and sea life usually travel around the country and don't spend so much time in Reykjavik, which is more of a cultural centre. But actually, there is lots of nature to appreciate, especially if you take to the open waters. Unlike many places, whale watching is a possibility through all twelve months of the year in Reykjavik, and whales are spotted on 90% of sailing expeditions.

7. Embrace Your Inner Fashionista

When you think of the fashion capitals of the world, places like Milan and Paris might spring to mind, but probably not the Icelandic capital. But you'll discover a whole new world of Icelandic fashion if you visit the Reykjavik Fashion Festival, which is hosted in March every year. As with every great fashion festival, the highlight is a series of glamorous fashion shows, but unlike the shows in New York and London, the public are invited to buy tickets and join in with the fun in Reykjavik.

(http://rff.is)

8. View the City From The Pearl

The Pearl, or Perlan as it is known locally, is one of the best loved buildings in Iceland's capital. On the ground floor, there are 10,000 cubic metres of exhibition space, and it's a great space to take in concerts and live events. But if you want to visit in the daytime, be sure to head to the fourth floor where there is a viewing deck. From there, you have great views across the city, particularly when you utilise the telescopes on the deck.

(www.perlan.is/?lang=en)

9. Stroll Through a Sculpture Garden

Reykjavik is a wonderful city, but it's also kind of expensive, and if you are on a budget, you'll want to know the free attractions that the city has. Fortunately there are plenty of them, and the Einar Jonsson Sculpture Garden might just be our favourite. Einar Jonsson is a famous and beloved sculptor from Iceland, and this garden showcases many of his beautiful bronze casts. There is also a museum attached to the garden where you can learn more about the man and his art.

(www.lej.is/en/museum/garden)

10. Take a Summer Day Trip to Videy

If you have more than a few days in the Icelandic capital city, you may want to take the opportunity to make a few day trips outside of the city. Videy is the perfect choice – an island located in the Kollfjordur Bay, which is accessible via ferry. The island has some archaeological remains that date way back to the 10th century, and incredible bird life, with 30 species of birds breeding on the island.

11. Learn a Bit of Icelandic

When you visit a foreign country for the first time, it can be really frustrating when you can't pop to a shop or restaurant and say what you want to say to communicate with local people. Although the majority of people in Reykjavik can speak English, if you are sticking around for a while, it can be a great idea to learn a little of the local language. The Multi Kulti Language centre offers classes for all abilities, so there is no reason not to give it a go even if you are a total beginner. *(Barónsstígur; www.multimal.org)*

12. Party Hard at Airwaves Festival

For a small country with a small population, Iceland sure does know how to throw a party, and this is never more evident than at the annual Iceland Airwaves Festival. The festival last for 5 days every November, and it has been described as the hippest long weekend on the music festival calendar. Airwaves is dedicated to promoting new music from Iceland and internationally, and artists who have played the festival include Bjork, Yoko Ono, Hot Chip, and Metronomy. *(http://icelandairwaves.is)*

12. Catch an Icelandic Movie at Bio Paradis

Yes, when in Reykjavik it's certainly a great idea to check out all the local sights and museums, but there are times when all you want to do is lay back in a comfortable cinema chair and watch a movie. If that moment strikes while you're in Reykjavik, you should know about Bio Paradis. This independent cinema shows many art house films and it's dedicated to showcasing the works of Icelandic filmmakers. Fortunately, all movies have English subtitles so you'll be able to follow the plot.

(https://bioparadis.is)

13. Try the Bruce Willis Shake at Prikid Café

Fancy tasting a little bit of the city's history? If so, you should head to Prikid Café, which is the oldest café in Reykjavik, dating back to the early 1950s. This is a no-nonsense kinda place that is great for a lunchtime burger, but our favourite thing on the menu has to be the Bruce Willis shake. This is a milkshake with a shot of whiskey to give you the pick-me-up you need after a day filled with sightseeing.

(Bankastrati 12; http://prikid.is)

14. Splash Around in a Geothermal Beach

When you head to Reykjavik for a long weekend, you probably aren't expecting to enjoy any beach time. But if you are a beach lover and you visit in the summertime, you can find golden sand and warm waters at the geothermal beach of

Nautholsvik. The beach was opened in 2001 and since then it's been a roaring success with over half a million visitors every year. You can also find hot tubs and steam baths there so you can turn your visit into a luxurious spa day. *(www.nautholsvik.is)*

15. Keep Warm With Winter Woolens

If you're visiting Iceland in the winter months, you will need to wrap up toasty and warm. But if you arrive to Reykjavik and realise that you are still a little chilly, fear not, because there will certainly be something for you to purchase at the Handknitting Association of Iceland. Their store is full of hand knitted items from jumpers to mittens, and everything is created with love and care. The woollens there would also make wonderful gifts for friends and family back home. *(Skólavörðustígur 19; http://handknit.is)*

16. Dance, Dance, Dance at Secret Solstice

What better way to experience the onset of summer with an awesome outdoor festival in Iceland's capital? This really is the festival to visit for anybody who is a music lover as the festival founders love all types of music, and it shows in the acts that play on the stages. You'll find everything from

Icelandic indie acts to huge global names - all performing to the crowd of over 10,000 who are out to have a good time with Iceland's spectacular landscape as a backdrop. *(http://secretsolstice.is)*

17. Learn How to Become Icelandic in 60 Minutes

If you really want to get to grips with Icelandic culture, you don't have to stick around in the country for months and months. Because Reykjavik can be an expensive city, most people are only in town for a few days, but you can fully learn about Icelandic behaviours and culture in that time by catching the popular "How to Become Icelandic in 60 Minutes" at Harpa. Throughout the comedy show, you'll learn exactly how to walk, talk, and act like a true Icelander. *(www.howtobecomeicelandic.is)*

18. Take in a Classical Concert at Harpa

Located in the Old Harbour of Reykjavik, Harpa is an absolutely stunning structure, with its mirrored surface reflecting the harbour and the sky. Primarily, Harpa acts as a concert hall and it is the home of the Iceland Symphony Orchestra. It's also an important centre for many of the festivals that occur in Reykjavik throughout the year such as Dark Music Days, Sonar, and the annual Jazz Festival.

(2 Austurbakki; https://en.harpa.is)

19. Chow Down at a Secret Pizzeria

When you visit Reykjavik, of course it's a great idea to try as much local food as you possibly can, but sometimes all you want is a slice of pizza, right? If you're a pizza fanatic, be sure to head to Hverfisgata 12. You won't see any sign above the door, but not knock on the door, and you will be let into a secret, family style pizzeria with slices to die for. They also open as a bar until 1am so you can wash down your slice with a cold beer.

(Hverfisgata 12)

20. Feel the Country's History at the National Museum of Iceland

Iceland is a country of contrasts. Take a look at some of the contemporary architecture and you will see that it is a city that is right on the cutting edge, but it's also a city with a long and illustrious history, and you can discover this history in the National Museum of Iceland. The museum was established in

1863, and since then the collection has grown and grown. Highlights include medieval engravings and artefacts from the settlement period.

(Suðurgata 41; www.thjodminjasafn.is/english)

21. Ice Skate on Tjornin Lake

Although Reykjavik is a capital city, it's a small place and there isn't too much hustle and bustle. One of the most popular places to relax is around Tjornin Lake, which is the most prominent lake in the city. It's a peaceful spot at any time of the year, but we particularly enjoy visiting in the dead of winter. It gets so cold in the winter time that the whole lake freezes over and its sturdy enough to be used as a public skating rink. Why not strap on your skates and join in with the fun?

22. Find Something Special at Kolaportid Flea Market

There is only one flea market that exists in Reykjavik, but with a flea market as amazing Kolaportid, more than one really isn't necessary. Located in the beautiful Old Harbour neighbourhood, you'll be able to find vintage clothing, second hand books, hand crafted items, hand knitted jumpers and mittens, and lots of knick knacks beside. It opens every weekend, and because its indoors you can enjoy the market right throughout the year.

(Tryggvagötu 19 , Old Harbour, Grófin; http://kolaportid.is/Index.aspx?lang=en)

23. Step Back in Time for the Viking Festival

When talking about ancient Icelandic history, the most well known period is the medieval era of the Vikings. Of course, it's possible to learn all about the Vikings in various museums across the city, but it's at the annual Viking Festival that ancient history comes to life. The festival actually takes place just south of the capital, in a village called Hafnarfjodur, and throughout the festival you'll find sword fighting, Viking concerts, and you can even eat in a Viking restaurant. The festival takes place in June each year.

(http://fjorukrain.is/en/about-the-festival)

24. Feel the City's Creativity at Kirsuberjatred

Whether you're in Reykjavik for a couple of days or a couple of months, you will no doubt want to take something home from the city that will always remind you of your trip. Trust us when we say that it's best to bypass all the tacky souvenir shops and to head straight for Kirsuberjatred. This is a trendy little shop where up and coming designers make items such as handbags made from fish leather and bowls made from vegetables, as well as many other quirky things.

(Vesturgata 4; www.kirs.is)

25. Have an Artsy Day at the National Gallery of Iceland

If you are an arts lover, you might think that a holiday in Paris or Florence would be best for you, and while these are wonderful art destinations, do not overlook Reykjavik. For arts lovers, a day at the National Gallery of Iceland is a day well spent. Founded in 1884, it contains a very impressive selection of Icelandic art, and if you really want to get to grips with the local arts culture, we would recommend splurging on a guided tour through the galleries.

(Fríkirjiuvegur 7; www.listasafn.is/english)

26. Party All Night Long at Paloma

Reykjavik might be a small city, but you'd never think that if you party there as it has a party scene that can rival any of the capital cities of western Europe. One of our favourite places to shimmy all night long is at Paloma. Electronica and pop is the order of the day, and you are likely to hear classic pop songs that you recognise, so there is no excuse not to show what you have on the dancefloor.

(1-3 Naustin)

27. Get Rude at the Icelandic Phallological Museum

Reykjavik has some fantastic museums, and if you are looking for a museum that is a little bit different, the city certainly will not disappoint you. The Icelandic Phallological Museum is dedicated to, you guessed it, everything phallic. And this museum is no small affair, it actually contains the world's largest collection of penis specimens for 98 animal species, including the penises of reindeers, foxes, rats, and more. Maybe leave the kids at home for this one, eh?

(Laugavegur 116; http://phallus.is)

28. Have an Awesome Cup of Coffee at Reykjavik Roasters

If you are the kind of person who can't function until you've had your morning cup of coffee, you are in luck because Iceland is a nation of coffee drinkers. In fact, the average

Icelander consumes 8.3 kilograms of coffee every year. While coffee is of a great quality throughout the country, we reckon that the very best cup can be found at Reykjavik Roasters. The café is a tiny size, but don't let that fool you – the coffee packs a major punch.

29. Listen to Smooth Sounds at Reykjavik Blues Festival

Blues music is a genre that you would probably associate with the Deep South of America more than Iceland, but if you love blues music, fear not because there is an epic blues festival every year in the Icelandic capital. The festival takes place in March or April, and it always launches with "Blues Day", which includes many blues performances outside in the town centre. Throughout the festival, you can find small gigs and major concerts all over the city.

(Brautarholt 2; http://reykjavikroasters.is/english)

30. Watch History Come to Life at the Saga Museum

The Saga Museum is one of the most unique museums in the country because instead of relying on artefacts behind glass screens to tell the country's history, it actually brings history to life. As you walk through the museum, you will discover wax people in various scenes that tell the story of the country's history. The displays are very graphic, and may not be for the faint hearted even if the blood is all fake!

(Grandagarður 2; www.sagamuseum.is)

31. Try a Local Food – Cod's Tongues

When you visit a new country for the first time, you probably expect to encounter new and strange foods that you've not heard of before, but we confess that we were a little thrown by the cods' tongues that you can find on the menus in Reykjavik. This unique delicacy is something of an acquired taste, but you cannot fault the commitment to using every element of the animal. This is one for food adventurers!

32. Discover the Works of Sigurjon Olafsson

Sigurjon Olafsson is one of the most famous artists to have emerged from Iceland, and he is particularly well known for his 20th century modernist sculptures. At the Sigurjon Olafsson Museum, which used to be the artist's studio, you can find a selection of sculptures, drawings, sketchbooks, and well as information about the man himself and his relationship with his country and how it informed his art. *(Laugarnestangi 70; www.lso.is/index_e.htm)*

33. Attend a Session in Parliament

Althingi is the word for the Icelandic parliament building, which is located in the centre of the city. As well as being a beautiful building that you may want to visit and photograph, it is actually possible to get a feeling for the local politics of the country by attending a parliamentary session. This is possible between the months of October to May, and the parliament opens to the public four times a week. *(Kirkjutorg; www.althingi.is)*

34. Sip on Icelandic Beers at Craft Beer Trinity

When you think of destinations around the world that are famous for their beers, Iceland is probably not the first country that springs into your head, but this is not to say that there is no brewing culture in the country. In fact, it is alive and well, and this will become very apparent if you pop your head into Craft Beer Trinity of an evening. This bar is dedicated to showcasing the wares of local producers, and we think you'll be pleasantly surprised by the country's output.

35. Discover Contemporary Dance at Everybody's Spectacular

For a festival that is a bit more interesting than beer, bands, and camping, you should definitely try out Everybody's Spectacular, which is an annual performance festival. You can expect cutting edge performance art in unique locations, talks and discussions with performance practitioners, as well as loads of parties where you can dance the night away with like-minded arts living individuals. It takes place in August every year.

(www.spectacular.is)

36. Watch A Nature Film in the Old Harbour

The Old Harbour is one of the most picturesque parts of the Icelandic capital. But as well as being wonderful for an evening stroll., it's also a great place to catch a movie. At a cinema called Cinema No 2, which is a converted warehouse in the area, you can watch an array of nature films. They have screenings about the country's volcanoes, about the Northern Lights, and more besides so be sure to keep up to date with their schedule.

(Geirsgata 7b; www.thecinema.is)

37. Discover the Local Photography Scene

If you have ever visited a photography museum, you'll no doubt find that it exists as a sidekick of other art museums, and the collections are not comprehensive. Not so at the Museum of Photography in Reykjavik, which contains a staggering collection of five million photographs that extend from 1870 to the present day. You'll find portrait photography, landscapes, commercial photography, family photos, and more. Altogether, the photos tell a very comprehensive story of the country.

(Grófarhús, Tryggvagata 15)

38. Take in a Concert at Salurinn

Although Salurinn was the first specially designed concert hall in Reykjavik, it actually opened less than twenty years ago. What it lacks in years, it certainly makes up for with very impressive acoustics. If you are really serious about music, this is definitely the place to catch a concert that sounds really fantastic. All kinds of music events are hosted in the hall, so whether you want to listen to a classical symphony or a modern rock concert, the choice is yours.

(Hamraborg 6, Kópavogur; www.salurinn.is)

39. Plaster Your Body With Silica Mud in the Blue Lagoon

The Blue Lagoon, a geothermal spa that lies not too far from Reykjavik, and it is one of the most visited places in the country for people who want to relax and pamper themselves while on holiday. At the bottom of the spa, you will find pure silica mud. On your visit, you can have mud mask treatments from this nutritious mud to exfoliate and moisturise your skin. And if you love that experience, you can also take some home with you from the Blue Lagoon shop.

(www.bluelagoon.com)

40. Enjoy Island Life on Grotta

When the local people of Reykjavik want to escape the city life and get back to nature, they head to Grotta Island on the weekend, and this could be a really magical day trip for you too. There really aren't a whole lot of major sights or attractions on the island, but that's part of the charm. This is simply the place to visit with someone you love, and to walk hand in hand with them while strolling on the beach and taking in some sea air.

41. Stroll Through Holavallagardur Cemetery

While wandering around a cemetery might seem like a somewhat morbid thing to do, we actually think that Holavallagardur Cemetery is rather lovely, and so does National Geographic who have called it one of the loveliest cemeteries in Europe. As well as the mandatory headstones, you will find an endangered species of moss over the stones, and there are birch, rowan, and willow trees throughout the space, which actually make this a very charming place to spend a quiet morning.

(Suðurgata)

42. Discover Medieval Manuscripts at The Culture House

If you are something of a culture vulture, don't miss the opportunity to spend a pleasant afternoon at Culture House. As the name would suggest, the institution is devoted to everything cultural. You can find manuscripts of medieval sagas from one thousand years back and at the same time you can look at contemporary Icelandic art. Through the exhibitions, you'll get a better picture of how Reykjavik transformed from a few scattered farms to the capital city it is today.

(Hverfisgata 15; www.culturehouse.is)

43. Get Explosive at Volcano House

Did you know that Iceland is one of the most volcanically active countries on the planet? Well, you can learn lots more about this interesting facet of the country at Volcano House. The highlight of a trip is watching one of the films that are shown every day. One of these covers the great eruption of 1973, which caused 5000 people to flee the small island where the volcano was spewing out lava.

(Tryggvagata 11; www.volcanohouse.is)

44. Watch a Play at the National Theatre of Iceland

If you love a reason to get dressed up in the evening, make sure that you know about the National Theatre of Iceland, which as the name would suggest, is the premiere theatre in the country. The playhouse puts on around thirty productions, which are extremely varied. One week you'll see a musical, the next an opera, and the next a piece of up and coming new writing from an Icelandic writer.

(Hverfisgata 19; www.leikhusid.is/English)

45. Tuck In to Rams' Testicles if You Dare

How much do you know about Icelandic food? Probably very little, and it's no wonder because Icelandic food isn't exactly an international sensation. But if you want to try something traditional and typical., there is one dish that you can't miss: rams' testicles. That's not a euphemism - we are actually talking about the testicles of a ram here. The testicles are boiled and cured in lactic acid if that makes them any more appealing.

46. Wave a Rainbow Flag for Gay Pride

Iceland is one of the most progressive countries in the world when it comes to LGBT rights. Same sex marriage was legalised in 2010, and gay couples have had access to adoptions services and IVF since 2006. The annual Gay Pride celebrations in Reykjavik, which take place at the beginning of August each year, are a way of celebrating everything that the community has achieved, and a way of pushing for further equalities. The highlight is a colourful parade that takes over all the city's main streets.

(http://hinsegindagar.is/en)

47. Get Yourself Some Hipster Threads at Leynibudin

Fancy yourself as something of a fashionista? Well, there are plenty of opportunities for shopping in Reykjavik, but the question is where is the best place to go if you want something really unique and special? We whole heartedly recommend Leynibudin, which you can think of as a minimarket that hosts all the up and coming designers from Iceland. Items border on hipster, which is no bad thing if you ask us.

(Laugavegur 55; https://leynibudin.is)

48. Get Artsy at the Reykjavik Arts Festival

Iceland is a small country with a whole lot of creativity, and the creative heart of the country can be felt every year at the Reykjavik Arts Festival. This festival is multidisciplinary, and it has a particular focus on new commissions and the intersections of different artistic media. You'll find performance art, pop-up exhibits, music shows, and more in the many cultural spaces around the city, as well as innovative spaces such as abandoned warehouses and factories. The festival takes place in late May or early June.

(www.artfest.is)

49. Raft Along the Hvita River

If you are an outdoorsy kind of person, a trip to Reykjavik is a must because you can combine the culture of a capital city with tonnes of outdoor adventures. One outdoors experience that we particularly love is rafting on the rapids of the river Hvita. This is a glacier river, and on a rafting expedition, you can experience the beauty and the force of Iceland's natural wonders first hand. There's a mix of rapids for adventure and calm parts of the river where you can simply relax and take in the vistas.

50. Watch Movies at the Reykjavik International Film Festival

If you are a cinema fanatic, make sure that you coincide your trip with the Reykjavik International Film Festival, which takes place every September. The festival has a real commitment to showcasing the works of up and coming Icelandic film makers so don't expect any Hollywood blockbusters. But if you are interested in the craft of cinema and like the idea of making some creative discoveries and attending small screenings and Q&A sessions, this will be right up your street.

(www.riff.is)

51. Trek the Esjan Mountain

If your idea of a great vacation is not hopping from museum to museum but actually getting active and immersing yourself in the landscape, there are numerous places for a breathy hike in and around Reykjavik, and we highly recommend the Esjan Mountain. This mountain is often called the city mountain because it totally dominates the city skyline. There are many well marked hiking trails that cater to different fitness abilities, so there's no excuse not to get hiking even if you're a total beginner.

52. Get Musical With Dark Music Days

Reykjavik has a very strong festival culture, and one of our favourites is Dark Music Days. While most festivals are hosted in the summer months, winter travellers can join in with the fun of Dark Music Days as this festival is hosted in the middle of winter, at the end of January. The simple but effective idea is that contemporary musicians are given a platform in the stunning Harpa Concert Hall. Beautiful music in a beautiful venue – what could be better?

(www.darkmusicdays.is)

53. Purchase Handmade Shoes at Kron

Whether you are a woman who loves to shop for shoes or you have such a woman in your life, you need to etch in some time to visit Kron on your visit to Iceland's capital city. The shoes inside are handmade, and there are many colourful styles, which will really make you stand out as you walk down the street. For shoe lovers, Kron is a candy store with an endless supply of treats, so why not indulge?

(Vitastigur; http://kronkron.com)

54. Be Wowed by the Northern Lights

The Northern Lights are known as one of the most spectacular natural phenomena in the world, and it's possible to see the Northern Lights for yourself on a trip to Reykjavik. While many people choose to visit the city in the summer months when it is a little bit warmer, you are actually better off visiting Reykjavik in the dead of winter if you want to see the Northern Lights, because they are most visible when it is cold and dark.

55. Have a Unique Dining Experience in a Rotating Restaurant

Reykjavik is a city with an incredible array of restaurants, but perhaps the most special of them all is a restaurant called Perlan, which is located inside the building of the same name. The reason why this restaurant is so special is that it rotates. As the restaurant turns around, you'll have an epic panorama of the whole city – and what's more, the food served up there is pretty special to boot.

(www.perlan.is/?lang=en)

56. Discover the Country's Seafaring Heritage

As an island, Iceland has a very strong history of fishing and shipping, and indeed, this is still big business in the country. At Vikin Maritime Museum, which is located in a former fish factory, you can learn all about this part of the country's coastal culture. You'll be able to see ships that served in the recent Cod Wars right up close. The Cod Wars involved a series of confrontations between the UK and Iceland about fishing rights in the Atlantic.

(Grandagarður 8; http://borgarsogusafn.is/is/sjominjasafnid-i-reykjavik)

57. Play Board Games at Babalu

Babalu is one of the most iconic cafes you'll find in Reykjavik, and the reason is simple – it is packed full of charm and style. The place has a very local feel, and that makes it a great place to connect with local people and make new friends. It's made that much easier because there are many board games available for you to play in the café so you can ask somebody who catches your eye if they'd like to play a game with you.

(Skólavörðustígur 22; www.bablu.is)

58. Sip on Quality Cocktails at Loftid

Reykjavik may have a reputation as an expensive city, but it's still important to indulge now and then, and what better way than with a delicious cocktail with a loved one in the evening time? For cocktails, we recommend Loftid, which is decorated beautifully with mannequins and sewing reels located around the bar. This is definitely a place where you will want to dress up and enjoy the opulent city at its best. *(Austurstræti 9; www.jacobsenloftid.is/en)*

59. Embrace Contemporary Art at Reykjavik Art Museum

If you are looking to have an artsy day in the capital, waste no time and head straight to Reykjavik Art Museum. And this is no place to spend just a half hour or so as it's the largest art institution in all of Iceland. There are actually a few different locations of the museum around the city, and we particularly like the museum at Hafnarhus, which contains lots of works by the Icelandic pop artist, Erro.

(17, Tryggvagata; http://artmuseum.is)

60. Take in a Soccer Match at the National Stadium

It's fair to say that soccer is the most popular sport across Europe, and in Iceland that is no exception. If you fancy seeing a soccer game for yourself while you're in the country you can head to Laugardalsvollur, which is the official national sports stadium in the country. The stadium has a total capacity of 15,000 and it's where all the international matches are held.

(www.ksi.is/mannvirki/laugardagsvollur)

61. Make the Most of Happy Hour at Bravo

It is no secret that Iceland is an expensive country to visit, particularly if you want to have a few alcoholic beverages in the evening time. Thank goodness that you have us to let you know about the best places for a cheap drink. For our money, Bravo is absolutely the best bar for a cheap drink that's also high quality. The happy hour lasts between 6:30 and 9pm every day, so there are plenty of hours to fill yourself up with booze.

(Laugavegur 22)

62. Have a Local Experience with Couchsurfing

It is no secret that Reykjavik is an expensive city to visit, but is it possible to do it on a budget and to have a great time? It sure is! Sign up to the Couchsurfing.com website and you will find lots of local people who have spare beds or couches and can offer you some space for a few days. Not only is this a great way to save money – it's also a wonderful way to experience a genuine cultural exchange and to get to grips with the real life of locals in Reykjavik.

(www.couchsurfing.com)

63. Be Wowed by the Icelandic Dance Company

If you have an interest in the contemporary arts, you'll want to know all about the Icelandic Dance Company, who have been credited with pushing the envelope for choreography in Iceland, and putting Iceland on the global dance map. The dance company has been putting on shows since the 1970s. As they are based in Reykjavik's City Theatre, that's the place to go if you want to catch one of their spectacular shows.

(http://id.is/en)

64. Enjoy Delicious Veggie Food at Dill

If you are vegetarian and visiting Reykjavik, there is no need to despair at the amount of protein that people eat to warm themselves up in the cold temperatures the island experiences, because you can always have a delicious veggies filled meal at the wonderful Dill Restaurant. The chef is also a champion of raw food so if you are looking for some food that is healthy, innovative, and delicious all at once, it's the place to be.

(Hverfisgata 12; www.dillrestaurant.is)

65. Get Back to Nature in Reykjavik Botanical Gardens

For peace, tranquillity, and lots of greenery, there is no better place to pass the time than at Reykjavik Botanical Gardens. It's here that you will be able to find more than 5000 subarctic plant species, and strolling through the grounds really gives you a sense of how incredibly diverse the flora of the northern temperate zone is. There is also a café on site, which opens from May to September, and cooks up treats made with ingredients from the garden.

(Hverfisgata 105; http://grasagardur.is)

66. Enjoy the Reykjavik Winter Lights Fest

During the city's winter months, Reykjavik is a very dark place to be, but that doesn't mean you should avoid the city at this time – far from it. At the end of February, one of the most spectacular winter festivals in Iceland takes place, the Reykjavik Winter Lights Festival. This takes place every year at the end of February, and the basic idea is that the city is illuminated with a beautiful light display, and there are cool arts events all around the city's various cultural venues at the same time.

67. Discover the Best of Iceland's Restaurant Scene

Love food? How about fun? Well, you'll find the perfect mixture of both at the Food and Fun Festival, which is hosted in Reykjavik at the beginning of March each year. The idea of the festival is that world renowned chefs are invited to collaborate with local restaurants to create spectacular dishes. There is also a competition that tests chefs' culinary talents as they are challenged to cook with local Icelandic ingredients exclusively.

(www.foodandfun.is)

68. Sip on Icelandic Whiskey, Floki

If you are serious about whiskey, you will want to try some Floki, the local whiskey brand, while you are in the country. Actually, Floki is not technically a whiskey but a malt because it is only kept in a cask for one year. And if you are an eco-friendly whiskey lover, you have even better luck because the distillery is totally powered with the country's geothermal energy, and the harsh winters there act as nature's pesticide!

(https://flokiwhisky.is)

70. Feel Serene at the Imagine Peace Tower

Do you love The Beatles? You might not think that there is any trace on the band on the island, but you would be mistaken. John Lennon's widow, Yoko Ono, has actually created a memorial to her late husband in the city. The Imagine Peace Tower is essentially a long tower of light on top of a white stone monument, which has word "Imagine" etched into it. Yoko chose Iceland for the monument because of the beauty of the country and its commitment to geothermal energy.

(http://imaginepeacetower.com)

71. Feel Iceland's Creativity During DesignMarch

Reykjavik is a contemporary city that exists right on the cutting edge, and you'll be able to feel that innovative creative spirit with huge force at the annual DesignMarch festival. The festival covers all aspects of the design, so whether you are in the market for some graphic artwork for your living room, a piece of innovative ceramics, or some fashion forward threads from Iceland, you'll find something that floats your boat.

(www.icelanddesign.is)

72. Discover the Street Art of Reykjavik

In order to get to grips with the arts culture of any city, it's important not to restrict yourself to see exhibitions in museums but to actually keep your eyes open and look at the art work that exists all around you on the city streets. Unfortunately, the government has recently cracked down on unauthorised street art, but you can still see many murals on the buildings of business owners who offer their permission. The best way of understanding the ideas behind the street art is to join one of the organised street art tours in the city.

73. Take a Seaweed Bath at the Peace Garden

With the gorgeous geothermal pools of Iceland, there are plenty of opportunities to pamper yourself on a trip to Reykjavik, but if you fancy doing something a little bit different, we wholeheartedly recommend a long bath in a tub full of seaweed in the Peace Garden. The seaweed in the area is said to have many beneficial properties for hair and skin, and it will be particularly useful if you have a dry complexion.

74. Listen to Experimental Sounds at Sonar Festival

Sonar Festival labels itself as a festival of advanced music and new media art, but for us it's simply a really fun party. The festival originated in Barcelona and now tours around the world, and Reykjavik is one of its preferred locations. This is the festival for you if you are interested in more experimental music and other forms of art. It takes place in Harpa Concert Hall in February each year.

(https://sonarreykjavik.com)

75. Learn About Reykjavik's Settlement Age

For a glimmer at the Reykjavik that existed many centuries ago, be sure to spend a day exploring the wonderful Reykjavik 871+/-2, which is the city's settlement museum. The whole museum is site specific and based around a 10th century Viking longhouse, and the museum is extremely engaging with a mix of modern technology and ancient artefacts. A highlight is an interactive panorama of how the longhouse would have looked back in the day.

(Aðalstræti 16; http://borgarsogusafn.is/en/the-settlement-exhibition)

76. Get Musical at the Reykjavik Jazz Festival

When you think of jazz music, it is very unlikely that you think of Iceland or Reykjavik at all, but actually there is a very

healthy jazz culture in the city, and this is very evident at the annual Reykjavik Jazz Festival, which takes place every August. Over the last few years, the festival has continued to build in size, and it is now considered to be one of the best jazz festivals on the international circuit. You'll find a mix of local Icelandic jazz performers and worldwide talent who are all united by their passion for the jazz genre.
(http://reykjavikjazz.is)

77. Chow Down on Minke Whale Meat

Do you love to try new and adventurous dishes when you visit a new country? Well, you have more than a few options in Iceland, and something that you might want to add to your to-eat list is the meat of Minke whales. Of course, this is somewhat controversial, and there are many activists who are opposed to eating this kind of meat. But if you are on board, a restaurant called 3 Frakkar is the place to tuck in. It has a very meaty taste and is not particularly fishy.

78. Say Hi to the Animals at Reykjavik Zoo

If you have ever visited a zoo before, you are probably used to seeing animals like elephants, lions, and giraffes in their various enclosures, but the Reykjavik Zoo is something altogether different. The focus here is on local animals and you'll find many wild native species. Some of the animals you will find include reindeer, seals, turkeys, cattle pigs, and many others besides. There is a petting schedule every day, which is always popular with little ones.

(Hafrafell v/ Engjaveg, Laugarnesvegu)

79. Find Vintage Treasures in Spuutnik

If you are something of a shopaholic, visiting a new city to discover all of its stores is probably high on your to-do list. But when you are new in a city, it can be difficult to know where the best places to grab something really special are. Well, if you are into vintage threads, we can totally recommend Spuutnik. This vintage shop has been around for aeons and it's the go-to place for anybody with a quirky sense of style in the city. Why not be one of them?

(Laugavegur 28)

80. Have the Best Burger of Your Life at Hamborgarabullan

Yes, when you visit a new city it's a great idea to chow down on all of the incredible local food, but there are times when all you will want to eat is a juicy burger. Right? Well, you're in luck, because against all the odds you might just have the best burger of your life at a restaurant in the city called Hamborgarabullan. It's the simplicity of the place that really shines through. You won't even be given a menu. You'll simply be presented with an amazing burger, and that is that.

(Bíldshöfði Bíldshöfða 18; www.bullan.is)

81. Make New Friends at Kex Hostel

If you're in Reykjavik for a while, you'll want to make a few friends. Kex Hostel is the place to do so for a number of reasons. First of all, as a hostel it will obviously be where you'll meet other travellers like you. But more importantly, this hostel is actually a bit of a hipster hangout with visitors and locals alike. Every night of the week you can catch something different, whether it's a live band or a movie night, and you can guarantee that it's always teeming with people who want to chat to new faces.

(Skúlagata 28; www.kexhostel.is)

82. Learn About the Icelandic Currency

Learning about Icelandic currency may not be at the top of your Reykjavik hit list, but if you do have some spare time on a cloudy afternoon in the city, we can highly recommend a trip to the Central Bank of Iceland. The collection there includes the full range of the currency as well as coins and notes from the past. The total collection contains five thousand types of banks notes and more than twenty thousand coins.

(www.cb.is)

83. Purchase Some Interesting Spirits at 64 Reykjavik Distillery

Every country has its own type of alcohol. You have vodka from Russia, tequila from Mexico, and port from Portugal, but what are the unique types of alcohol that you can sample on a trip to Iceland? We highly recommend touring 64 Reykjavik Distillery to find out. They have a range of spirits that are infused with very Icelandic flavours. We highly recommend the blueberry, rhubarb, and crowberry liqueurs for something a little bit different, and they make fantastic bases for innovative cocktails.

(www.reykjavikdistillery.is)

84. Enjoy Live Tunes at the Innipukinn Music Festival

If you want to dip your toe into the festival circuit without having to commit to a huge festival where you have to camp and spend a small fortune on the ticket, Innipukinn Music Festival in Reykjavik is a really awesome festival for beginners. The festival also takes place in various venues around the city, so it will always be protected from Iceland's unpredictable weather, and it's paired up with street food events for the more gastronomically inclined.

(http://innipukinn.is)

85. Explore a 3D Map of Iceland in City Hall

While Reykjavik's City Hall is an impressive building to visit and take pictures of in its own right, most of the visitors go there for one thing – the very impressive 3D map of all of Iceland that is contained within the building. The 3D map is made to scale, and you'll have the opportunity to explore many of the incredible geographical features of the countries, such as its volcanoes and lakes.

(Tjarnargata 11; http://reykjavik.is/stadir/radhus-reykjavikur)

86. Eat Deliciousness at Reykjavik Street Food Market

Needless to say, the temperatures can be on the chilly side in Reykjavik, but this doesn't stop the local population from heading outside and finding food on the street. The Reykjavik Street Food Market opens every Saturday in July and August, and you can find all kinds of deliciousness there – from tacos to Chinese buns, from lobster rolls to French fries. Yum!

(Tryggvagötu 19, Old Harbour, Grófin; www.kolaportid.is)

87. Take a Selfie by the Sun Voyager

One of the most iconic fixtures on Reykjavik's cityscape is a sculpture called The Sun Voyager, which was designed by Jon Gunnar Arnason. The idea of the sculpture is that it is a "dreamboat", which represents new voyages and hopes for the future. It is located on a small headland that looks out into the ocean, and it's the perfect spot for a peaceful for a moment or, indeed, a selfie with the iconic monument.

88. Explore the Red Rocks of Heidmork

Reykjavik is the kind of capital city that even people who are allergic to tall buildings and city traffic can get on board with.

It's a relaxed place and there's plenty of nature in and around the city. One of our favourite spots for a springtime hike is at Heidmork. This is an area of wild, forested parkland, and the highlight of a walk through these woods is the stunning bright red rock that exists there – a very striking contrast to the normally cool tones of the Icelandic landscape.

89. Take a Stroll Around Reykjavik Harbour

Reykjavik is the kind of city where you don't need to have a plan of attack. You can simply stroll along the city streets and you will have a wonderful time. And one of the most picturesque spots for a stroll is the harbour area. As well as being able to look at the many colourful boats docked in the harbour, this area plays host to many important attractions in the city such as Harpa Concert Hall. It's also a wonderful place to grab a bite to eat with a view.

90. Take it Easy in Dillon's Beer Garden

If you are not the biggest fan of cold weather, it's highly advisable that you visit Iceland in the summer months. While you are not likely to find any tropical temperatures in the Arctic north, you will at least have some sunny and bright days, and what better way to pass a sunny afternoon than in a beer garden? Our favourite spot for an alfresco pint is at Dillon's. It is filled with live music fans in the evenings, but the highlight is really the beer garden, which opens in the summer months.

91. Try Your Hand at Fishing

As an island surround by water, Iceland is a great place to try your hand at fishing, whether you are a first timer or you are an accomplished fisherman. There are plenty of tour companies who can offer you the opportunity to be taken out on the open waters, and to take part in sea angling from on board. You could catch fish such as catfish, cod, haddock, and mackerel, and afterwards you can even barbecue your own catch for a delicious fish supper.

92. Drink Brennevin, Iceland's Signature Spirit

If you are visiting Iceland during the winter months, you will almost certainly require something that can warm you from the inside out, and what better than the national tipple, brennevin? Although brennevin is not something particularly well known outside of the country, it's a big deal in Iceland. This spirit is a clear, unsweetened schnapps, which is flavoured with the distinct taste of caraway seeds. It is traditional to drink this with shark meat if you fancy double the gastronomic adventure.

93. Explore Iceland's Music at Reykjavik Midsummer Music

Want to experience beautiful music in a beautiful concert hall? Of course you do, and that's why you need to know about Reykjavik Midsummer Music, a festival that celebrates the diversity and creativity of the Icelandic music scene. The festival is also inspired by the 24 hours of daylight that occur at the time of the festival, which takes place every June. It's Harpa, the incredible concert hall that stages all of the festival performances, and the sublime acoustics of the venue make the music stand out for all the right reasons.
(http://reykjavikmidsummermusic.com/en)

94. Chow Down on Traditional Blood Pudding

When in Iceland, do as the Icelanders do, right? Well, if you want to have the authentic local experience, you'll have to chow down on the local food, and that includes a traditional variety of blood pudding, which is called blodmor. Try not to be put off by the whole "blood" thing because this local food is actually super delicious. It's typically made with lamb's blood, suet, and oats. It's best eaten fried with some dense rye bread.

95. Indulge an Inner Bibliophile at the Reykjavik Literary Festival

When you think of literary cities, your mind will probably wander to places like London or Dublin, but Reykjavik has an impressive creative culture, and that includes a decent number of writers. Actually the Reykjavik International Literary Festival has been held for more than thirty years and it's one of the most respected literary festivals in Europe. It's hosted every September, and during the festival you have the chance to meet authors, get books signed, and attend live readings.

(http://bokmenntahatid.is/english-2)

96. Fill Your Stomach at the Weekend Food Trucks

The food truck craze is so pervasive that it has even reach secluded Iceland! That's right, even with Iceland's chilly temperatures, hordes of locals are willing to brave the elements to chow down on something delicious. There are lots of food trucks that open in the old harbour area, and we are particularly fond of Lobster Hut, which serves up warming lobster soup and filling lobster sandwiches for a casual taste of what Iceland does best – fresh seafood.

97. Watch a Daring Theatre Production by Vesturport

If you are interested in the arts but you'd rather see an edgy new play than a classical symphony, you need to know about the local Vesturport theatre group, which is well known for creating edgy, innovative plays. Their plays are often very physical, and their fresh approach has attracted a new set of Young Icelanders to the theatre. They have even won the coveted Europe Theatre Prize, which has previously been awarded to the likes of Harold Pinter and Peter Brook. *(http://vesturport.com)*

98. Climb to the Top of Mount Keilir

Reykjavik is a city that has it all – tonnes of cultural attractions, amazing restaurants, and breath taking nature. If it's being outdoors that makes you really happy, one hike that you can do in just two to three hours is to the top of Mount Keilir. While this volcanic mountain isn't so high, it is very steep, and your fitness will definitely be put to the test when climbing to the top. Fortunately, the view from the peak offers quite the reward.

99. Get Festive at Reykjavik Christmas Market

While many people avoid Reykjavik in the winter months because of the cold and dark, we think that that is an epic mistake, particularly in the run up to Christmas when the city becomes very festive indeed. During this time, the whole downtown area transforms into a Christmas village with mulled wine, festive culinary treats, and entertainment for the kids as well.

100. Find a Bargain at the Red Cross Store

If you are stuck for something to do on a cloudy day in Reykjavik, why not hit the city streets and do some shopping? While prices can be high in Iceland, you'll be pleasantly surprised if you venture to the Red Cross Store in the city. If you are into vintage friends, this is the place to visit, as you can find awesome used clothing at reasonable prices. And better yet, all of the proceeds go to the Red Cross.
(Efstaleiti 9)

101. Indulge in a Luxury Dinner at Torfan Lobsterhouse

We know that Reykjavik can be an expensive place to eat out, but what is a trip away if you can't at least be a little indulgent? If you can only eat out in one fancy restaurant during your time in the city, make sure that it's at Torfan Lobsterhouse. The dish to have is, of course, the Icelandic lobster, and this classic hasn't changed in the restaurant for 25 years. It is simply grilled and then brushed with garlic butter, and it couldn't be better.

(Amtmannsstígur 1; www.torfan.is)

Before You Go…

Hey you! Thanks so much for reading **101 Coolest Things to Do in Reykjavik**. We really hope that this helps to make your time in Iceland the most fun and memorable trip that it can be.

Keep your eyes peeled on www.101coolestthings.com, and have an awesome time in the Icelandic capital.

Team 101 Coolest Things

CPSIA information can be obtained
at www.ICGtesting.com
Printed in the USA
LVOW07s1544170517
534871LV00010B/703/P